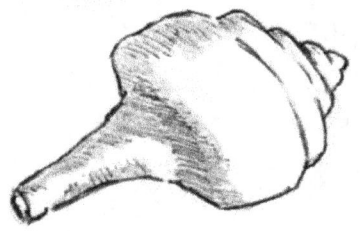

The Keeper of the Shell

Eileen Bell

Illustrations by Norma Hoyle

The Keeper of the Shell

By Eileen Bell

Illustrated by Norma Hoyle

Copyright Eileen Bell 2019

All rights reserved.

No part of this book may be used or reproduced in any manner whatsoever without written permission except in the case of brief quotations embodied in critical articles or reviews.
This book is a work of fiction. Names, characters, businesses, organizations, places, events and incidents either are the product of the author's imagination or are used fictitiously. Any resemblance to actual persons, living or dead, events, or locales is entirely coincidental.

ISBN 978-1-989092-31-6

Celticfrog Publishing, Kamloops, BC

About the Illustrator

A self-taught, frequent portrait artist, equally at home with oils, acrylic, water-colour or pen and ink, N. E. Hoyle's love of animals and nature, coloured most of her work over the years. To help illustrate this story however, after many years of left-brain work, she came out of retirement and drew on the skills learned in a cartooning course, which she says has happily reactivated the right side of her brain.

Other Published Works by Eileen Bell

Children's Books
Morton's Muddle- 1992,1998
The Keeper of the Shell- 2019-Celtic Frog Publishing
Available on Amazon in hard copy or e-book
Soft cover available from Ingram Spark Publishing

Works in Anthology's
Short Stories- Polar Expressions Publishing- 2015-16
Poetry- Polar Expressions Publishing- 2013- 2016

Poetry Books
Eileen Bell and Friends- Overland Press-2017
   River-land and other Poems- Celtic Frog Publishing-2020
Available on Amazon

Eileen Bell is a regular contributor of stories and poems to the New Author's Journal- Mario Farina-Publisher-Quarterly Journal
Available on Amazon in hard copy or e-book.

For other soon to be published works please refer to CelticFrogPublishing.com/Eileen Bell.

Sea-Shell

Sea Shell, Sea Shell,
Sing me a song, Oh Please!
A song of ships and sailor men,
And parrots and tropical trees,
Of fishes and corals under the waves,
And seahorses stabled in great green caves.
Sea-Shell, Sea-Shell,
Sing of the things you know so well.
                                        Amy Lowell

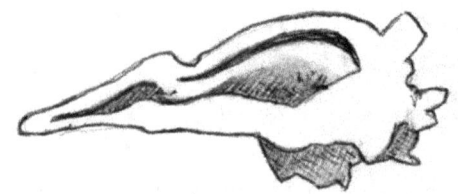

Chapter One – Iona makes a Discovery

Iona lived on a lonely island where a baked mud and grass hut was her only shelter. Two smiling dolphins brought her fish and kelp each morning. She plucked fruit and drank sweet juices from the two mango trees that flourished on the small island. She did not want for anything.

Iona felt her life to be without beginning or end. She sat by the shore and spoke out over the waves to the sky or mist or a squawking jay, not caring about who listened.

"My life is as mysterious and fathomless as the depths of the ocean. I don't know why I am here all alone. I am one with the sand and the sea but who am I?" She felt her destiny to be connected in some way to the endless ocean. She could not say this out loud however, as it bewildered her.

One morning as Iona was waiting for the dolphins, she picked a mango for breakfast. She spied a silver conch beneath one of the mango trees. One end of the shell was narrow with a curved indentation, which she blew into.

As she blew, the shell made an irritated, squawking sound as bits of sand flew from the mouthpiece. She tried again and this time out came a joyful tune.

I can't believe this. It's as if it's making music just for me.

Soon Iona could play the most beautiful tunes with little effort. Sometimes at twilight when the moon was rising and the tide rolling in, she would dance along the shoreline to the hypnotic music she created by blowing into this strange shell. Her long hair, as thick and tangled as seaweed and her tattered dress leapt and spun about in the cool ocean breeze, as if they too were answering the call of the haunting music and the endless ocean. She danced far into the night until she dropped exhausted on the sand, and the conch fell from her hand.

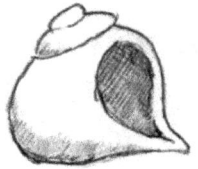

Chapter Two – A Visitor Arrives

Her sea friends would answer to a piercing note she created with the horn. Following this call were oddly patterned fish with stinging tentacles and saucy parrots from across the sea. Arriving at her shore were tiny birds with polished beaks, who picked between the crevices in the rocks for tiny morsels. She gazed in wonder at the tiny seahorses rocking on the crests of the incoming waves.

One night a fierce storm blew from the sea. She was picking a mango for her dinner when she saw the waves crashing against the shoreline. With the waves an assortment of fish and tiny seahorses were blown helplessly onto shore. *Oh no, I have to help them.* She began throwing them back in the water, but soon despaired, as they were blown back onto shore again on top of the huge waves. Iona fought the wind, refusing to give up.

In the distance something strange approached the shore. It looked like a large horse with a dazzling white unicorn's horn atop its head. As the creature pulled itself on to shore, water poured, then drizzled from his grizzly mane and flanks. Iona stepped back to make room for her odd visitor.

Before she could say anything, he spoke.

"Charlie Horse, Missis." He bowed his head and dripped water on her cold bare feet. She stepped back again. "Sorry, I been comin' a while. Saw you struggling with them little fishes, tryin' to get them back in the water. Awful storm, let's get to safety." Iona led him to the grass hut.

"I want to save my friends," she protested, staring out into the storm's fury.

"Ya' see that shell you been using to call them creatures? Stand outside the hut, facing the ocean, blow on the horn nine times, wait a few minutes, then blow another five times and watch what happens."

Iona was astounded, that he knew more about how to use her shell than she did, but she somehow trusted him.

Walking outside and blowing softly on the shell, she saw the waves crash less wildly against the island. Watching from the window of Iona's hut, they watched the sea return gradually to a more restful state. The creatures were no longer being thrown onto shore or being thrashed against rocks by the crashing waves.

Charlie had managed to crouch through the doorway of the hut and huddled in the corner drying out. Iona gave him a snack of dried seaweed. Iona was quiet while Charlie ate. She looked at him admiringly "How did you know this use of the shell, Charlie?"

"I know many things, I am an old seahorse who has travelled many miles and seen and understood many people and places. I may know many things, but only you have been given this mysterious gift of the silver shell and only to your call it will respond."

"But, why me, alone here on this island. Why has this shell found me?"

"I do not know, and I cannot tell. I must swim away now, dear child."

"Don't go Charlie."

Afraid he would say too much, Charlie hastened towards the calmer sea.

"I will be back to visit, as now we are friends and there will be many more stories to be shared. Your fish friends can go about their business again, thanks to you and your shell and I must go about mine."

To Iona's delight Charlie did return to visit. He often came ashore. She would cling to his long mane while they rode up and down the narrow shoreline. He spun tales of the sea and lands beyond. Charlie loved to talk, as a sailor who had been too long at sea. One sunny day he tried to warn her of the dangers of the sea.

"I have ta' tell you, Iona my dear, there are trolls that live down deep there in the sea in a spiked and mossy cavern fit for no decent creature." So taken was Iona with her new friend and his tales of handsome princes and shining castles, that she paid little heed to stories about monsters of the deep.

She had never had a friend to talk to, so when Charlie was away, she felt parched like a lost child wandering in a desert. Staggering along the shore as if in a drunken stupor, she would cry out to the waves. *Am I to be alone always? Is this my hollow fate?* She danced for long hours on the shore to quell her loneliness. When Charlie visited, she drank in all the warmth and companionship she could.

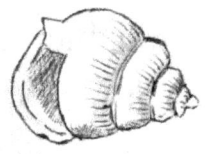

Chapter Three – An Unexpected Flight

Iona was sitting on shore one afternoon pondering again how she came to possess the shell. A thick fog lay across the sea. Suddenly, a large golden butterfly emerged from the mist. In spite of its size, it landed gracefully at Iona's feet.

She had no power to resist the lure of this painted lady, so without hesitation, but still clutching her precious shell, she rode out over the sea on the back of the butterfly. Wind blew against Iona's thin frame. Holding the shell tightly as a good luck charm, she fell asleep on the back of this winged insect.

She awoke suddenly, the force of rushing water pulling against her. Her eyes open wide in horror, as she saw she was being pulled down to the depths of the sea by a lurid glowing, green caterpillar. The insect had wrapped itself around her in a vice- like grip. She tried to wriggle free, but it was no use.

In a moment of horrible lucidity, she cried out from the depth of her soul.

"I am being taken to the lair of the trolls. If only I'd listened more closely to Charlie. What will happen to me now?" The shock of her capture and the cold water overcame her, and she and she sank limp into the caterpillar's grasp. As they passed the seaweed beds, beside the troll's mossy mausoleum, the silver shell fell from her hand.

She woke sometime the next day in a watery cave. She rubbed her eyes and looked about. Slimy snakes were creeping in and out of a circular pool of sea water in the middle of the musty den. *So I am a companion for water snakes now? This is my destiny?*

The hollow echo of her thoughts, voiceless in the nameless pit, drifted through her mind. She laughed bitterly at her foolishness at being brought to this putrid hole and the bottom of the sea. Then she gasped. *Where is my shell?* She grabbed the folds of her dress frantically and then stood and searched the floor of the cave looking for the shell she already knew in her heart the trolls had stolen. *My shell, the trolls have snatched my shell. Oh, where is my beloved shell?*

Head in hand, she slunk into a bleak fog of pain and confusion. Time became a blur. After several hours, her mind slowly began to question again what had happened. *Why did the butterfly capture me? What use am I to the trolls without the shell? Where are the trolls? I must escape this death dungeon.*

Chapter Four – The Fish-Man

Not ready for defeat, she found her way to the main floor. An eerie quiet surrounded her. A one-eyed troll guarded the only exit. She could feel his cloudy gaze on her back. She shuddered and slipped out of sight behind a doorway. She wandered through a twisted mass of tunnels, until she came upon a back room where a man lay on a bed of moss.

He seemed to be in a sleeping trance. His body was almost completely covered in a mass of fish scales. She was so entranced by the beauty of this man's unblemished face, she could not take her eyes off him. She knelt beside him and reached out her hand to touch his cheek, but caution drew her hand away.

Why is he sleeping in this nasty hole? Is he under a spell? Is he one of them?

Unsure what to do, she retraced her steps back to the cellar.

During her many dark hours in the snake pit, Iona began to notice an assortment of curious looking fish which sometimes swam in the snake's pool. She paid them scant attention, as always in the back of her mind was the thought of escape. The thought of the icy water outside the caves made her think again of what she was going to do. *To die here or in the frigid ocean is not much of a choice.* She would ask herself this question many times over as she pondered her dreary existence.

One ray of light was the sight of an ungainly, sea turtle who brought her food each night. He wobbled into her cellar each night on his short stubby legs bringing her delicate minnows or perch on a silver tray. He gave her a seaweed concoction to drink. It looked revolting but tasted sweet and delicious.

Iona was miserable and lonely during her long hours in the dungeon. She began talking out loud to keep herself from going crazy. She noticed the fish who swam in and out of the sea water pool.

"I can tell myself I am talking to the fish instead." She felt a shiver creep up her spine, from the shock of hearing her own voice through the cave's hollow reaches. Then from her mouth came an unexpected and bitter laugh. The hollow ring of her laughter echoed again through the tunnels of the cave.

As she sat deep in despair, she gradually began to notice a type of fish that was a beautiful marine blue. When a snake threatened it, it would turn into a round spiky blue and white ball and would face the snake with an open menacing mouth, mimicking the snake's hiss. Threatened by the protruding spikes, and this strange hissing fish, the snakes would back off. So they lived beside each other in an uneasy co-existence.

One night the turtle brought her two seahorses for dinner. "It's a rare delicacy ma'am, it surely is."

One glance at the tray and she grabbed it from his hand and threw it against the wall. She turned her face to the opposite wall, away from her only friend.

Turtle calmly picked up the tray and remains of dinner and as he left, he said,

"Will that be all madam?" Still turned towards the wall, she smiled despite herself at the

Turtle's persistence. Despair and loneliness overtook her that night. She lay awake haunted, unable to block out the hissing of the snakes.

I wonder if I will ever see Charlie Horse, or my tiny seahorse friends again.?

After the ill-fated offer of seahorse for dinner, she tried to keep her mind on memories of her larger sea-horse friend, but her mind kept drifting to the fish-man in the back room.

Iona sat as usual moping by the pool. "What am I to do? Maybe if I talk out loud long enough a fish will talk back." To her surprise she heard a voice that sounded exactly like her own. She looked around and a beautiful, blue puffer fish was standing upright beside the pool, rubbing his head with his long fin.

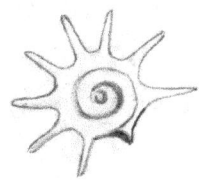

Chapter Five – Quack Helps Iona find her Way

"I'm Quack," he said holding out his fin for her to shake. She tried to hold onto his fin, but it slipped out of her grasp. He leaned back against the wall, rubbing his head again with the same fin. Under his dorsal fins she could see he had legs and feet like a person. His feet were flat and were shaped like a pair of shoes that were too big. "About time you stopped feeling sorry for yourself. If I can mimic those stupid snakes didn't you ever think I might be able to talk just *like* you and also *to* you?"

"I never thought." Iona was flabbergasted. "Maybe you will be able to help me leave this place one day soon."

Quack leaned closer and then said, "Anytime you want to talk." His mouth formed into an odd twist as if he didn't know whether to laugh or cry.

Then he laughed and it rang out just like the hollow and sad way she often laughed. This amused her, but she did not respond. Instead an escape plan was hatching in the back of her mind.

One night, not knowing her own intentions, Iona drifted down the maze of tunnels to the fish-man's room. She shook him gently, but he did not wake. Trembling with weakness of body and spirit. She took refuge beside this man on the bed of moss. *I wonder what color his eyes are? Are they deep blue like the ocean?* This was her last thought before falling asleep.

In a dream their minds linked. She told the fish-man of how she came to be in the troll caves, and he told her of a beautiful castle and land on the far shore, that he was destined to reign over one day.

In the morning, she felt refreshed but could remember nothing they had said in their dream. She knew their minds had met, so she found herself beside the fish-man again the next night. This time he urged her to escape.

"I will be fish food for the trolls soon. My scales are thickening." He described the silver castle once more. "You must swim to the silver castle on the far shore. Be brave and soon you will know all." He would say no more.

The next morning, she remembered all the fish-man had said. She was sad to leave him, but she knew it was time to escape. The knowledge that the fish-man was really a prince, and also that Quack could imitate voices, helped her see there was a way out and perhaps another life waiting for her. *Where I will live and who or what I will be is unknown. All I know is I must leave this horrible place.*

She no longer had just herself to think about. She must escape and find Charlie. Charlie would know what to do. She knew her predicament was as much connected to fish-man, as it was to her.

Later she idly watched an odd type of fish swimming in the pool. For the first time she noticed their deep shovel-like snouts. She began to wonder why it was that clean water was always in the pool. With hope awakened, she began to eat a little again each night. Once when turtle brought her dinner, she asked him,

"Why is the water in the pool always clean?"

"The shovel-fish, ma'am, they move the mud in and out with their snouts. Do you see the crack under the wall? Beyond that is the sea. and over the years the crack has become a hole large enough for a body to swim through. The shovel-fish create a mud-free tunnel by pushing the mud out in front so new seawater can flow into the pool."

Iona looked and for the first time, she noticed sea-water had worn away a chunk of rock from the bottom surface of the cave wall.

"It's a small hole ma'am, but the shovel-fish clearing the mud makes it easier to swim through."

Did he guess her intentions? She was not sure

she trusted the turtle.

"Thank you," she said quietly, not wanting to appear too curious.

"Will that be all Madam?" She smiled briefly and nodded at her friend. The tray swayed under his arm and as he ducked under the low doorway to make his exit, he turned to Iona. "Lester's the name Ma'am." He gave her a sly wink and then was gone.

All night and the next day she watched the shovel-fish come and go and by the early morning she had a plan. She would follow the shovel-fish out of the pool. She wished she could talk to them, like she could talk to Quack. She decided to ask him if he could stand guard and hiss at the snakes to keep them away, while she escaped through the bottom of the worn wall.

"My friends and I can do better than that," Quack told Iona. "We'll get the shovel-fish to move the mud right ahead of you, while you swim out into the sea. My puffer-fish friends all look just like me, but I am the biggest and smartest. They will create a babble of voices to confuse and scare away the snakes before you dive into the pool. I am without a doubt the best pretender, but all my friends can do a fair job." As he said this, his chest puffed out like a blue balloon. As he puffed himself out larger, his whole body became a round blue ball with small protruding white spikes. As Quack became rounder his flat, oversized feet and skinny legs became completely exposed. "See what I mean", he said, looking down at his odd, unfish-like body parts. "We have lots of tricks to scare away all the nasty snakes."

Quack thinks a lot of himself. Oh well, he is a puffer fish, maybe it comes with the name. She had forgotten to ask him to organise the shovel-fish, but before she could think any more about it, he was there telling her he had talked to the shovel-fish and they were ready to help.

"We'll do it tonight Quack, before I lose my nerve and with it, any hope of a life outside the cave."

At dusk, Iona paced beside the pool. The pool swirled with a mass of hissing snakes. They climbed over and under one another, in and out of the pool, hissing at her under her feet and trying to wind around her legs. "Get away you horrible creatures," She flailed and kicked at them in desperation. "Oh, I hope Quack shows up soon." She shuddered, as it was getting dark. She kicked aside another snake that was crawling at her feet. *It's as if they sense something is going to happen.*

A babble of voices startled her. She turned to see a circle of round, blue, puffer-fish with their white spikes lined up behind her, each singing a different, discordant tune and dancing back and forth on their flat feet, in a kind of comical, conga line. Quack, in his unpuffed state leaned against the back wall, watching what was going on.

A quick thought ran through Iona's mind in the midst of the chaos. *It's as if Quack has two personalities, maybe more. As many as he chooses!* As quickly as she could turn around, the shovel-fish with their bright eyes, appeared from nowhere and ignoring the snakes, began to tunnel mud underneath the wall and out into the sea. A rush of fresh sea water swept into the pool.

The startled snakes, confused by the babble of voices behind Iona, slithered through the line of dancing puffer fish. Quack made faces at them and mimicked their hisses, as they passed him to retreat to the darkest corners of the cave.

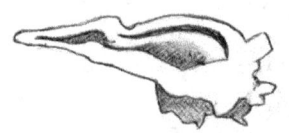

Chapter Six – Iona's Plans go Wrong

Iona stood shivering, facing her friends, standing ankle deep in the pool. Before she left, she waved goodbye and called out a grateful "Thank you, all you babbling, blue fish." She took one last look at Quack and his friends beside the pool and then plunged briskly under the water following the shovel-fish under the rock wall. They worked three at a time shoveling the mud ahead with their snouts. Iona had to fight the rush of sea water flowing back into the cave. As she emerged on the other side, the last thing she heard was Quack and the others in a chorus, mimicking the way she had said her goodbyes. *I will miss those odd characters,* she thought, as she shivered against the bone chilling cold of the ocean.

She needed to move away from the sea floor before she became food for the many creatures in the ocean. Energized by her new purpose, she forced her body upward, through the water to safety. Once on the surface she began to swim in what she thought was the direction of the far shore, but her energy had been sapped by her push to reach daylight.

Unaware of anything but her drive to reach the distant shore, Iona struggled on. Several trolls from the cave were swimming after her. She did not sense the danger until one was almost on top of her. They had spread out over the ocean to increase the chances of catching her. She was helpless against the one who found her. Though she shrieked as loud as she could, the troll was grimly intent on dragging her back to the cave and to her certain death. She screamed again and tried to wriggle out of his grasp.

Charlie, luckily, was at the surface entrance to the troll cave. From the surface of the water, no one would know where in the vast ocean marked the point at which to dive to the sea bottom. An increase in the warmth of the water and a slight difference in the water color was all there was to mark the spot. Charlie knew the place, as he had tracked the trolls for many years to keep other creatures from their harmful ways.

After Iona disappeared, he had spent his time searching the sea and talking to friends. As he had suspected, and friends had confirmed, she had been taken to the troll cave.

Just at that moment, he heard her screams echo from far across the water. He dove as rapidly as he could down to the sea bottom and the cave of the trolls to wait for the troll to return with Iona. *Thank goodness for the troll's poor vision. This gives me time to think how I can save her.*

The trolls had once possessed the shell Iona had found on the beach and had used it along with their own talents to create a unique world that harbored them and their kind. The trolls had also used it for evil purposes and so it had drifted away to find it's true and lasting home. In a sense, it had a mind of its own. Magic is hard to describe because it's just that - magic.

Charlie knew that the genius of the trolls lay in their engineering abilities. As he stood outside the cave he stood on flat ground and the ocean was suspended above him. In order to protect themselves from the dangerous waters, the trolls had little by little and with the help of the smaller, less troll- like gardeners, pumped away the water, until this magic bubble had formed around the entrance to the troll cave. Charlie's amazement never lessened each time he saw this spectacle.

This area is as beautiful and well-tended as the inside is rampant with stinking moss and weeds. A fungal mix had created spikes which grew from the cavern roof. Inside of the cave is ugly, dirty and disordered. Here I am surrounded by beautiful, flowering plants and vegetables of every kind. Trees that grow any manner of fruit. Almost anything one could wish to eat.

A short distance away lay a large pool of ocean water in which a number of turtles about the size of Lester were swimming contentedly.

One of the many green troll gardeners Charlie remembered seeing once or twice, spotted Charlie. He leaned on his fork and smiled.

"Good to see you again Charlie, but I know it's bad business or you wouldn't be here. We are a peaceful lot, us greenies as we're called. My name's Leif." He pointed to his mottled green face as he spoke. His eyes were a mottled green as well, except that from the pupil shone a clear almost translucent blue.

"Happy to know you, Leif. You are a different species from the trolls but somehow the same."

"We are sworn to secrecy otherwise…" Leif performed a slicing motion across his throat. "I can tell you this though," he whispered close to Charlie's ear. "We are neither male nor female, and yet we are both." He sniggered, slightly abashed at his confession.

The greenie picked up his hat from the ground, brushing the dirt away. "Hope one day you succeed, Charlie, bad business, bad business." He shook his head sadly and turned back to his work.

Charlie was surprised by the revelation that the greenies were both male and female.

Nothing should surprise me anymore. They are gentle creatures, so they are kept away from the main cave and made to work in the garden. They supply all the trolls need for food and yet are given nothing in return. They eat what they grow and make the clothes on their back from the workings of their own clever minds. Yet they remain so kind-hearted and gentle. I wonder what will happen to them when the cave is no more.

Charlie settled under a large lime tree with willowy branches flowing to the ground. Camouflaged by the green foliage, he waited uneasily for Iona. He pondered the tale of how Iona had struggled to escape through the rushing waters under the cave. Then he realized,

She was kept in the depths of the cave out of the reaches of the bubble. So when the cave was designed, they were thinking of ease for themselves on the top floor and death and destruction for their enemies on the bottom.

Charlie looked up to calm himself. The sea above was like a sky to the creatures of the deep. The sun rose as it did on the earth above each morning. Oxygen and light filtered through the bubble to provide sustenance and the regular cycles of night and day to the creatures on the ocean floor.

As he waited, he noticed something strange. Quack was standing just inside the main doorway, talking in an animated voice and waving his flippers excitedly and smiling nervously at a heavy troll.

The troll was dressed in a smart looking vest and short clean pants. The troll had a monocle over his right eye, and was bending over, peering through the eye-glass into Quacks face. He was speaking in a sharp, but uncontrolled garble and was spraying spit on Quack as he did so. A sinking feeling overcame Charlie. Then he overheard what Quack was saying to the troll. Quack backed away from the troll who kept coming closer.

"Yes, Yes, I know…I had to let her escape, I had no choice. I had to keep her trust and I could not stop her from leaving. I knew your trolls could easily snatch her back and then you would have no excuse not to do away with her. You have the shell, so why do you need her?"

"Because now she is not in prison. She has the freedom to find help to snatch back the shell. It's ours! It's ours!"

After this shower of words, Quack stomped his feet, then turned and stumbled, in his awkward rush to get away, over a crumbling rock in the doorway. He righted himself, fluttered his fins haughtily and mimicking the troll's odd speech, he stomped and fluttered down the hallway. The troll marched in straight behind him, still spewing his nasty garble at Quack.

Charlie was relieved when he saw the monocled troll and Quack go inside the cave.

Hopefully, I can somehow pry the troll away from Iona. His thoughts raced as he waited. Then he saw the creature from a distance, dragging poor Iona by his large grimy teeth, which gripped her dress by the neckline. He was dragging her off to the side of his slimy body.

As the troll neared the cave, Charlie surprised him by jumping out in front. He lay on his back in the water and his strong feet came forward and caught the large troll in the gut. Not only was the troll forced backwards across the water, a good distance away, but his gut was torn to shreds by the force of Charlie's hooves. He soon sank lifeless onto the ground, as his body still lay inside the confines of the bubble.

Charlie bent down beside Iona as she dragged herself, dripping and shivering, onto his back. Charlie swam past the outskirts of the bubble and up into the cold merciless ocean.

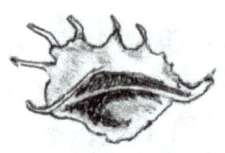

Chapter Seven – Home to the Island- Adventures at Sea

Iona was free. She lay across Charlie's back and clung to his neck, her heart pounding with relief

and gratitude. Charlie focused for a long time on swimming to safety. He finally spoke.

"We'll go back to your island home and rest

for a day or so and make our plans from there."

There was no time to lose as the other trolls who had heard the commotion were emerging from the cave waving their arms and shouting. They could easily have caused more trouble. Charlie's strong legs carried Iona swiftly home. When they arrived home, Iona sank onto her straw mat and didn't wake until Charlie nudged her, as the sun was rising slowly over the ocean.

Sitting beside the sea, they traded adventure stories. The dolphins brought them kelp and fish as before. It seemed as if as if nothing had changed for Iona while she was talking to Charlie and stroking the dolphins, but in reality, nothing was as before. Her destiny was no longer to be lived alone on this island. Her life was somehow tied up with the fish-man's life and with the new friends she had made.

"We must travel to the far shore and find the castle of silver shells, as Fish-man spoke of in our dream."

"Yes," Charlie answered, "the trolls have stolen the shell, as it alone possesses the power to unlock the door of the castle. The keeper of the shell is also the keeper of the castle, the land around it, and all that's inside its doors."

As Iona sat beside the sea eating fish the two dolphins had brought her, she remembered her fish friends in the cave.

"Seems strange to eat fish now Charlie, as I have fish friends who still live in the cave. Good thing that the fish I'm eating doesn't look like Quack, the puffer-fish who helped me escape or the shovel-fish who helped tunnel me out under the wall." Charlie looked down, so as not to show his worry, when she mentioned Quack. Inside he shuddered as he thought of Quack's betrayal of Iona.

Iona sat quietly and rubbed the dolphins' noses. They waved their flippers and swam away. "Why do they bring food and swim away so fast? They used to stay and play. Maybe it's because I no longer have my shell. Odd, it's almost as if I know them from another life." She looked at Charlie and saw something sad and knowing flicker across his face.

Charlie pawed the sand with his hoof. At last he spoke. "We must do as the fish-prince says and waste no time. We must have the help of the thornback fish if we are to drive the trolls from the castle." Iona climbed on his back and they sped away.

Thornback fish were called so, because out of their backs grew long thorn- like protrusions, which they could fling at will, like darts, to either stun or kill their enemies. They also had eyeballs similar to shovel-fish, but much bigger. They could project their eyeballs out of their heads, on a coiled spring, in order to see over long distances.

As they were as lazy as lizards when not patrolling the sea, Charlie found them basking in the afternoon sun on a tiny island near their destination. He spoke to them in one of the many varied languages of the sea.

While Charlie was busy with the thornback fish, Iona spied a prawn with beautiful blue grey iridescent wings, shuffling a shell in front of her along the shore. Struggling to keep up behind mom, were three tiny baby prawns. She could just see the tips of tiny wings beginning to show from the side of their small bodies. Mama prawn was trying to push a shell that was much too big for her. She kept pushing it backwards over her own head. The creature peeked out from the top of the shell and looked up at Iona.

"Using this shell for the roof of my house, very heavy. Got a brood here and trying to build a house safe from the tide." Iona picked it up and stared at it. She was amazed. It looked almost exactly like the silver shell that was stolen from her by the trolls.

"Why don't we find you a better fitting shell for your roof? This one is much too big." She pushed the shell under a willowy bush and helped the prawn find a smaller shell that fit, but first she helped her build a home from sticks, shells and seaweed and fashioned with a small door made from wet sand and kelp. "That should be a safe home for you, out of the way of the tides."

"I'm Peggy, Peggy Prawn. You with Charlie over there?"

"Does everyone know him?" Iona asked, trying to stay calm and not betray her surprise.

"In these here parts, he's known for fighting with those trolls. Been trying to get them out of that castle for years." She pointed with a claw to the far shore and a misty castle barely visible as it was shrouded in fog.

"How strange for the castle to be hardly visible through the fog, but not the land around it." Iona retrieved the shell from under the bush. She was anxious to rejoin Charlie.

"Where you heading?" Peggy asked, as though she already knew.

"Just looking for shells with Charlie." Iona was trying hard to sound casual. "Mind if I take this one?" Iona held up the shell.

"No use to me now you helped me build my house. Long way to come for a few shells, I'd say. I'm known in these parts for keeping a shrewd lookout."

Seeing that Peggy was not easily fooled, Iona

changed the subject.

"Perhaps you'll fly away soon," she said looking at Peggy's wings. Peggy looked sadly at her fairy-like wings.

"Been stilled; these wings - just stopped working a while ago, strangest thing."

Iona left quickly. "Thanks lady, come back and visit me and the family," Peggy called after her.

What strange creatures I am discovering. Imagine meeting puffer-fish with legs and feet like humans and winged prawns that can't fly. What's next? As she climbed on Charlie's back, her mind was whirling with ideas. She hid the shell under her cloak, not wanting Charlie to see it just yet. She was planning an idea to rid the castle of its trespassers.

As they reached the coastline, Iona spotted two large trolls patrolling the shoreline. By this time night was approaching. The thorn-backs, whom Charlie had rallied as an army, were swimming with them to the castle. Suddenly they vanished under the water.

At a short distance from shore, two poison thorns shot noiselessly, up and out over the water and into the stomachs of the two Trolls killing them instantly.

Charlie said to Iona, "We will creep near the

castle and let the Trolls see us close by the window. I am too big for them to miss seeing me, so I will easily lure them outside and the thornbacks will deal with them from there."

Chapter Eight – The Keeper of the Shell

The castle was as Iona had seen it, when she was united in her dreams with the Fish-man. A shell and sandstone castle with turrets made of spiral and spindle shells, round shaped windows, opening over the sea, fashioned from the finest grains of salt-sand, vast meadows and gentle green mountains stretching behind.

    Charlie and Iona rested hidden beside a wide-spreading tree in full bloom which was laden with luscious, ripe strawberries. Through a small side window Iona could spot a troll with a crown of seashells hanging sideways off his head, talking in a non-stop gibberish and drinking from an earthen goblet.

    "That's Nebula, King of the Trolls," Charlie whispered. "He's the one who put the spell on the prince and also on you, so you would be entranced by the butterfly. He has your shell. He must be destroyed, as the other Trolls will be lost without their leader."

Iona looked determinedly at Charlie. "I am going in inside alone to face Nebula," she stated firmly.

"You have been in enough danger already, Iona. You are the key to all that has happened. Please, please do not go in there alone, Missis. I brought the thornback so they can finish off the nasty trolls."

"I will need the thornback and you later, but I have a plan to trick the King of the Trolls into giving up the silver shell without a fight. You and the thornback can deal with him as you like, when I have the shell back safely in my hand. Charlie, you need to trust me with this plan."

Charlie pawed the ground anxiously and then looked up at her.

"This is dangerous, and you could get hurt." It was no use to say anymore, so Charlie thought of another way to help. "The thornback and I will lure the trolls from the castle before you go in. The trolls have not seen you yet, so please wait here until we have dealt with most of the trolls." Then he turned and walked towards the largest window in the castle.

One of the Trolls, lurched forward spilling his

drink, lifting his goblet towards Charlie and then turning to alert the others in a language Charlie could make no sense of. As the fat, drunken Trolls spotted Charlie, they stumbled, jabbering, from the castle. The beach was soon littered with the bodies of dead trolls, their bellies struck with poison darts.

Iona, in truth, didn't have any plan. King Nebula and a few of the trolls that had likely gone to hide were still inside. Iona knew the shell she had found on the tiny island was somehow connected to her shell, as a kind of companion or sister shell.

I could try blowing on it and see what might happen, she thought, *but there is no time to experiment. I am hoping this new-found shell will know the whereabouts of the original shell. First, I must convince Nebula he has the wrong shell. If my plan fails, what will we do then? Is Peggy, the winged prawn, the keeper of this shell? If this is so, why did she let me take it so easily?*

Iona sat beneath the strawberry tree until it was completely dark. One of the thornback fish quietly approached her. They also had human legs and feet, like the puffer-fish, that they could use on land as needed. He said no words, but immediately she understood that with his bright pop-out eyeballs he would be her lantern in the night.

"Thank you for coming to help me, but please, no poison darts for the King for now. I need to talk to Nebula." The thornback did not answer but seemed to understand. He led her ahead through the dark night. As they entered the castle, through the main door, he turned down his lantern eyes.

They saw everything that had once been beautiful in a shabby broken and dirty state. *No time to think about this. I must find the King.* She found him dozing, his head hung over the side of his golden chair with his crown still somehow attached to the side of his head, his mouth hanging

stupidly open. The goblet had fallen from his thorny hand. The shell was nowhere to be seen. A small ripe strawberry was lying on the table.

She picked it up and popped it in his open mouth. He spluttered and woke up spitting the strawberry across the room. The thornback stayed, listening through the door-jam. Nebula sat staring at Iona in disbelief.

I must take a chance while Nebula is still in shock. She gasped and her heart thudded against her chest. She took the shell slowly from under her cape and put it to her mouth. It began to play a mournful tune of lost love which, to her astonishment, put Nebula in a trance.

He got up and began to dance slowly around the room in his short, rough garment, his fat legs swirling, his chubby arms outstretched as if around a partner, in a romantic dance. He muttered in a silly gibberish, totally unaware of his surroundings. She lay the shell down on a table and it continued playing. While Nebula danced, her eyes were directed to a cupboard at the end of the room.

"Keep playing the tune, little shell." She spoke loudly. The cupboard was locked. She looked pleadingly at the shell. It changed its tune to a short staccato and the lock fell from the hinge to the floor.

At the moment the tune changed, Nebula changed from acting out his silly dance, into a death like high stepping march and began to walk straight ahead, arms swinging, as if to march through the front door. Instead he turned sharply, walked towards an open window and hoisted his legs up and over the sill.

The problem was he could not get his oversize gut through the window. He was stuck, hanging comically, half in and half out of the window. He kept trying to pull up his head and chest to grab onto the sill above, but his head and chest kept falling backwards inside the window frame. He was like a short sausage caught in a very undignified pose. It took several thornback and their deadly darts to finish off the King of the trolls.

Iona could hear Charlie snorting, whining and prancing about on the ground outside the window. *He better not celebrate too soon, There could be still a few trolls inside the castle.* Meanwhile, as Iona looked inside the cupboard, she saw her shell, lying on the top shelf.

Chapter Nine – The Prince and Lester Take a Journey

Iona picked up the shell. She blew on it twice. Prince Andaman instantly awoke from his long trance, deep in the troll's lair. Scales fell from his body and scattered to the floor. He stretched and smiled.

"The spell has been broken, after these many long lonely years."

The caves and all the evil creatures who lived in it, along with all the trolls crumbled into dust and were washed away by the sea. The bubble dissolved and with it the beautiful garden the Greenies had so lovingly tended. It evaporated as easily as a soap bubble on a sunny afternoon, but not until Lester and Andaman had passed by its borders.

The Prince and Lester, who had always been the Prince's faithful companion, were at last free to choose their own destiny. The Greenies, led by Leif, climbed on the backs of the half dozen turtles from the pool and decided to follow Lester and Andaman away from their crumbling home.

The shovel-fish who had helped Iona escape, swam away into the vast ocean.

Andaman climbed on Lester's back and Lester's carried his Prince up through the cold sea to home and friends waiting on the far shore. They saw the Greenies swimming up through the sea beside them, perhaps to follow them to the castle or to find a kinder garden to tend on one of the islands along the way.

"I am happy the kind, green trolls are free," Andaman confided to Lester. "All the good creatures can now find new lives, just as we are doing."

Several of the Greenies and their turtle companions did happily find a refuge on Quack's island home along the way. Leif and another Greenie decided to take a risk and journey with Lester and Andaman to the castle beyond.

Chapter Ten- Revenge and Discovery

Quack was spared, but only partly, from the revenge of the shell. His followers were also spared from becoming part of the crumbling dust that had become the troll cave. They were forced by that fateful moment when Iona blew two short, sharp notes on her shell in the far-away castle, to spend their remaining days on a remote island.

As the castle crumbled around them, and gravity returned once more to cover all of the sea bottom, they found themselves swimming with Quack in front, towards a remote island, by a force beyond their control. Quack tried to keep control of what was happening, but each time he tried to swim in a different direction he was pulled back on track to the remote island.

"Where are we going and why?" he shouted over the waves. The waves taunted him with a deep, shimmering echo. This startled him into silence. Quietly he cursed the force beyond his control. *What have I come to when the great sea mimics me? My so-called cleverness*, he was forced to admit during his lonely solace on the island, *has brought pain and hardship to others.*

So he began to help others rather than outsmart them, although on occasions when danger threatened, this ability to outsmart proved useful. The remote island soon became a place which welcomed other creatures in need of refuge. Quack learned to look kindly after those who arrived at his shore, and so redeemed himself. He was still inclined to boast of his own deeds, but never again tricked his friends.

"We welcome all who come onto our shore," he would say to the bedraggled creatures who sought refuge on the island. In truth, he was rather tired of his own kind and longed for new company. One day a lobster dragged himself onto shore.

"Tired of the sea for a while, Think I'll try life on shore. Seems like a good place to rest. Course, I don't rest much. Name's Harry, if you don't mind my company for a bit."

Quack was surprised, but quick to reply. "Yes Harry, I'm Quack. Be our guest Harry, anything you need, We'll not anything, Ah-- yes- Harry. What do you eat?"

48

As if reading what was on Quack's mind, Harry answered.

"I eat from the sea, small creatures and bugs and so on. You are too big for a meal. Harry put out a clawed hand to pat Quack on the back, as a joke between friends, but Quack stepped back. "Ye-ss," Harry grinned widely showing a mouth full of tiny, sharp pointed teeth. He crunched himself into a woven grass chair. "I play a good tune if any of your kind care to dance." With that Harry drew a miniature fiddle from a crack in his shell and proceeded to play a short tune. Harry held the fiddle between his shells on either hand, and with his claws bouncing over the strings, he stepped to a lively tune. He drew a crowd of puffer-fish who began to stomp their large feet and sing along.

He soon became a dear friend and all the puffer-fish began to look forward to his visits. So the long period of loneliness ended for the colony of puffer-fish. They could sing and dance with Harry the lobster. He was amused by their wish to mimic his speech. The Puffer-fish even taught Harry to mimic them! They all would roll on the beach and shriek with laughter as they copied each others' way of talking.

Meanwhile, on the small island where Iona had met the winged prawn Peggy, she spoke to her children.

"Look, look my little ones, my wings are working again." Peggy flitted back and forth across the island. The babies tried to spread their immature wings in imitation of their mother. "Not yet my children, but soon." She smiled at their efforts to copy her. "I know now the spell has finally been broken and when your little wings are strong enough, we will all fly to the far-shore and see for ourselves how Iona and her Prince have fared since she left here. While she was here, I knew that things would begin to change once she realised the connection between the two shells. I played a small part in helping this story unfold and soon we will all be proud and happy to join her and her friends at the castle."

Iona was thrilled to have her shell back in her possession. She wanted to dance on the beach, as she had long ago, but she felt like a different person now. Instead Iona blew on the shell twice to call her dolphin friends to pull the trolls bodies into the water. They helped her happily and she thanked them, but this time they didn't swim away. They cavorted and played near the shoreline.

"Maybe they are expecting visitors," she said to Charlie. "Do they know what I do not?" She blew twice more on the shell, the castle doors opened, and a fresh breeze blew through the halls, as in thankful response to its new occupants. Iona was puzzled as she understood the castle belonged to the Prince. Charlie watched this transformation from the water's edge.

"You are brave and kind, he said to Iona. Life will be treatin' you well now, I expect. No trolls bothering you and all. My life is not here with you. It is helping others on the wide-open sea as always. Goodbye for now, Missis."

"Oh Charlie, you are the dearest friend. How can I thank you?"

"You helped to rid the sea of the trolls and all the creatures that live here will be grateful to you. You have made my work easier. What will I be doin' with no trolls to hunt?"

She threw her arms around his neck weeping.

"Never mind Missis, I'll be back soon." Wiping tears from her face, Iona watched his strong frame grow fainter as he swam away into the far ocean. She kept her eye on his clean white horn, which reached upward like a shining, beacon from his head, until it too faded into the grey mist of the ocean.

Chapter Eleven – Iona Learns the Secret

The dolphins brought a breakfast of sea shrimp. Iona sat by the shore and watched the two companions tumbling about in the water. She gazed out to sea and couldn't believe her eyes. She saw, in the distance, the Prince riding towards the shore on Lester's back. *Am I seeing things? I can also see two trolls riding on turtles behind them. Why would the Fish-man dare to or even want to bring trolls with him to this beautiful shore?*

The Greenies waited near the edge of the water awaiting Iona's response. Andaman stepped on shore, where he knelt and bowed before Iona.

"We meet face to face at last. I am Prince Andaman. You have broken the spell of the troll, Nebula, saved my home and my life."

Iona was at once shy and astonished. Blushing and stammering, she answered, "Fish

Prince... Yes Andaman, whe-ere are your scales?" Then she spoke in a sterner tone. "Why do you bring trolls to our shore? They must leave at once."

"My scales are no more, just as the troll and their cave are now dust in the sea. This evil is banished. The shell is key to many mysteries and has brought *us* together. As for these trolls, they were the gardeners of the troll cave. They are gentle and kind creatures, not at all like their nasty cousins. They wish to be of service as gardeners to you in your new home. May I tell them they can come ashore? I am the Prince of this Castle and land."

Iona was drawn to Andaman who was kneeling in front of her in the sand, but felt a cold shiver run down her spine, at the sight of the trolls waiting by the edge of the sea. She was thrilled to see the Prince free from harm, healthy and strong standing beside her. This confirmed her belief in herself, her friends and what they had all done to save Andaman and the good creatures of the sea. Still, she did not want to give in easily.

"Have them come ashore. They can make their home in the cottage out back. Lester can help the greenies settle in and look after the turtles. I don't know how much time the turtles will spend on land, but Lester can sort their living space out with the greenies."

Andaman bade the Greenies come ashore and Lester greeted his friends. As Leif and his friend approached Iona she drew back, but she could see their manner was humble and kind as Andaman had said. They bowed, each in turn to Iona.

"Thank you for allowing me and my friends to come ashore, Leif said, as he bowed to Iona. We'll do our best to be of help to you here in your beautiful, seaside home. We have all been through a difficult time. Life will be better now for all of us. Two more of my kind are staying to help out on a far-away island where Quack and his puffer-fish friends have been given a new home."

She raised her eyebrows in surprise but did not reply.

The Greenies bowed again and turned towards the cottage behind the castle. Although the turtles did not speak as Lester did, Iona saw they walked as he did, awkwardly, on their small feet. She watched as they followed the Greenies. Lester walked in front of the turtles and behind the greenies carrying a small crinkly leather bag, held up high between his two short front flippers, his back feet mincing forward like the steps in an overdone dance recital.

Iona was shaken and overwhelmed by many emotions. Thoughts and feelings swirled through her brain. The emotion she felt most strongly was love for all the creatures, but most present was her love for Prince Andaman.

"I was once so alone and now all sorts of creatures are arriving at my shore wanting to help." *I am the keeper of the shell*, she thought to herself, realising fully for the first time her rightful place. She felt a flush across her cheek. Recovering, but still shaken, she looked mockingly at Andaman.

"You'd better get off that one knee in the sand or I might think you are asking to marry me."

Now it was the Prince's turn to be taken by

surprise. He stumbled to his feet. Standing very close, he stammered.

"I jus-ust might be—ahh yes, I might."

Iona looked up, relieved to have a distraction. She pointed to the sea.

"Look, Lester is swimming with the other turtles and the dolphins."

Their laughter rolled and spun out over the waves as they watched their friends play, but in their hearts, they wondered about what had just happened and what was to come.

Chapter Twelve – A Wedding and A Reawakening

A few weeks later Andaman and Iona were married and began their life together in the castle. On a lazy morning, a few days after the wedding, Lester arrived at the door with breakfast. "For a fine Prince and his beautiful Princess, who used to live so alone, shrimp and seaweed cakes, made by baking them in a pit under the hot sun. A change from Sea-horse Ma'am, if I can say so without you flingin' a plate." He chuckled. Iona was taken by surprise, as she had rarely seen Lester's playful side.

"You'll be dancing with our dolphin friends next."

"Been frolicking in the sea with them this last evenin' while you were sleeping, my lady." As he left the room, he passed a shrewd look toward Andaman.

The next morning, as a soft awakening breeze blew from the water, Andaman asked Iona to play two short shrill notes on the conch, as she usually did to call the dolphins.

When she walked outside, she found an old man and woman sitting side by side in woven chairs facing the castle.

"Oh Mom and Dad, you've come back. You've come back! My life is complete." She hugged them joyfully.

Surprised by all the fuss, they only smiled and nodded. They had lost all memory of the time they were enchanted and lived as dolphins, unable to protect and care for their child. King Nebula had put them under his spell to live as sea creatures, so the unfolding of the destiny of Iona and Andaman would not come to be.

Life for the old couple was now as if the past had never been, and the present was all they had ever known. Iona and Andaman, after the rediscovery of Iona's parents, made a promise to each other to remember the lessons of the past, but to live each day, fully in the present, as her wise and loving parents were now doing.

Many friends shared time with Iona and Andaman at the castle. Peggy and her children visited as soon as the small prawn children were old enough to make the journey. Peggy and Iona became as close as sisters. They would laugh and joke that the shells were sisters in thought and feeling, and so had brought them together as sisters. Different in species and appearance, but one in heart. Charlie was a regular visitor. Lester, the two turtles and the two Greenies stayed in loyal service to Iona and Andaman for the rest of their days.

Iona and Andaman were blessed with two children, first a girl and then a boy.

One evening at sunset, Iona watched as her little girl spun in a wild dance beside the sea, as she had long ago.

I remember my childhood days. I am so grateful that my children will not have to spend lonely days beside the sea as I did. She seems so like me, this young dancer. She will have adventures of her own one day.

The End

www.ingramcontent.com/pod-product-compliance
Lightning Source LLC
Chambersburg PA
CBHW050508240426
43673CB00004B/150